Aug 24

love your
library

Buckinghamshire Libraries

Search, renew or reserve online 24/7
www.buckscc.gov.uk/libraries

24 hour renewal line
0303 123 0035

Enquiries
01296 382415

follow us **twitter**

@Bucks_Libraries

CAROLE NAOMI MITZMAN

The girl on the
STATION

A STORY OF SURVIVAL AND SELF-DISCOVERY

MEREO
Cirencester

Mereo Books

1A The Wool Market Dyer Street Cirencester Gloucestershire GL7 2PR
An imprint of Memoirs Publishing www.mereobooks.com

The girl on the station: 978-1-86151-821-7

First published in Great Britain in 2017
by Mereo Books, an imprint of Memoirs Publishing

Copyright ©2017

Carole Naomi Mitzman her right under the Copyright Designs and Patents Act
1988 to be identified as the author of this work.

The address for Memoirs Publishing Group Limited can be found at
www.memoirspublishing.com

Cover Design - Ray Lipscombe

The Memoirs Publishing Group Ltd Reg. No. 7834348

The Memoirs Publishing Group supports both The Forest Stewardship Council®
(FSC®) and the PEFC® leading international forest-certification organisations. Our
books carrying both the FSC label and the PEFC® and are printed on FSC®-certified
paper. FSC® is the only forest-certification scheme supported by the leading
environmental organisations including Greenpeace. Our paper procurement policy
can be found at www.memoirspublishing.com/environment

Typeset in 12/18pt Century Schoolbook
by Wiltshire Associates Publisher Services Ltd. Printed and bound in Great Britain
by Marston Book Services Ltd, Oxfordshire

Printed on FSC approved paper

CONTENTS

>-+-+>-+-O-+-<+-+-<

Chapter 1

Evacuation

>━┤◆>━○━<◆┤━<

They say a person cannot remember further back than the age of three and a half. I was about that age when in 1939 my sister and I were put on a train along with a large number of other children from London to be evacuated to the country.

I can't remember being put on the train or saying goodbye to my mother, but I do vaguely remember my sister Anita holding my hand while we were dragged around for hours as the district nurse who accompanied us tried to find someone to take us in. I was crying, hungry, tired and frightened. Some people said they would take in the older child (my sister), while others said they would take in the younger one (me), but nobody wanted both of us. Fortunately the district nurse was aware what an extra trauma it would be for my sister and me to be separated, and she insisted we should stay together.

Initially we were taken in by a couple in West Hyde, but according to my sister they were unkind to us and I used to hide under the table because I was afraid. I don't know how true that is as I don't remember it, but whatever happened, we were taken away from them after just a few months. Nor do I remember arriving at Maple Cross, but that's where we ended up. Maple Cross was a very small, countrified place then with just one shop and a pub, and like most of the evacuees my sister and I hardly had any clothes, so we were given second-hand clothes that had been donated through the war effort. Also, each morning I was given a large spoonful of cod liver oil and malt, which was handed out to every child who was considered undernourished.

Mr and Mrs Coster, the couple who took us in, were decent Christian people. They had a son, Ray, who was about the same age as me. Although they took us in, fed us and gave us a home, they never showed any real affection. However in time I came to think that they were my real parents and called them 'Mummy' and 'Daddy'.

There were a few other evacuees at Maple Cross and their parents used to visit them regularly, but ours hardly ever came. I can remember once when my foster mother said 'Your mother is coming to see you tomorrow, so we must make you look pretty'. I couldn't sleep with excitement, and in the morning my foster mother put me in a new dress and curled my hair and took my sister and me to the railway station at Rickmansworth. We waited eagerly for the train to come in and watched as everyone got off, but she wasn't on it. Disappointed, we waited for the next train and the next, but she wasn't on any train, so eventually we went back home with me sobbing. I wet the bed that night and many nights afterwards, as waiting at the station and watching the trains for my mother who didn't turn up happened on quite a few occasions.

Although she didn't come to see us, she did always send us presents at Christmas and birthdays, or so I thought – I wasn't aware then that the presents were actually from my foster parents.

Of course, as a little child I couldn't have known what a sacrifice the Costers must have made by taking us in. They were not rich people and because they now had two extra children to take care of they never had a holiday, or a life of their own. For my foster mother the burden was even heavier, as there were no mod cons then, no washing machines or vacuum cleaners or fridge freezers. Milk, meat, butter and so on were was kept on a cold slab in the larder and only stayed fresh for a couple of days, so she had to cook every day. Heavy washing like bed sheets and towels had to be boiled in the copper tub, rinsed by hand in the sink and wrung out on an old mangle before being hung out in the garden. The toilet was outside next to the coal shed, which had no light, so we had to take a torch with us when we needed to use it.

Once a week all three of us children would take it in turns to bathe in a tin bath using the same water, which was rather unfortunate for the last one. Life must have been so hard. I could never have done what they did, and I wish they were still around so that I could let them know how grateful I am for them giving up their lives for my sister and me.

With all the trauma of separation, the war and trying to fit in, it's funny that the things you remember are the simple things, like on a Sunday when my foster father would go across the road to the pub for his pint of beer, and my foster mother would say to me 'Go and tell dad that his dinner is ready'. And I remember the old man who used to come once a week, pushing a cart and ringing a large bell, and how my foster mother would give me an enamel bowl and send me to buy a pint of winkles for tea. We mostly lived in the kitchen, which always smelt wonderful, as there was usually something cooking in the oven of the large black range, which was always alight. The front room was only ever used when visitors came, or on special occasions like Christmas, when friends and relatives of my foster parents would all gather around the old piano and sing carols. Some of the grown-ups would also join in games like pass the parcel, or musical chairs. For my sister and me it was a happy time, in spite of the war.

On Saturdays, my sister and I were sometimes trusted to take the bus to Rickmansworth to buy sausages from the butcher that my foster mother always used. Even with rationing and the scarcity of some foods we always managed to eat well, because my foster parents grew all their own vegetables and kept chickens, so we always had fresh eggs. I used to feed the chickens and gave them all names, and one Christmas when I found out that the dinner centre piece was one of our chickens, I burst into tears and refused to eat it. I still can't bear the thought of killing animals to eat.

Although the war didn't touch us much in Maple Cross, I can remember seeing the barrage balloons in the sky when I walked home from school, and at night we would look out of the window to watch the searchlights looking for enemy planes. Very often the sky would be lit up like fireworks. It all seemed very exciting to us children – we had no idea that people were being bombed out of their houses in London and that hundreds of men, women and children were being killed or injured. I would pray each night that my parents would not be hurt.

My foster father was a volunteer in the Civil Defence and he used to go around all the houses to make sure that the blackout curtains were drawn and no lights could be seen. He had built a huge concrete air-raid shelter at the bottom of the garden, and as soon as an air-raid siren sounded, we would all rush down there in our pyjamas and slippers. It wasn't very pleasant as it was dark and always smelt damp, and there were spiders and sometimes frogs sharing the shelter with us. Sometimes we would hear Doodlebugs (V-1 flying bombs) going over making the strange pulsing, buzzing noise they made, but we would be glad we could hear the noise because we knew that if it stopped it would fall to the ground and explode.

One of the brighter episodes of the war was when the Americans arrived in England. All the kids in the neighbourhood would wait on the side of the road for the jeeps to pass by and scream out 'Got any gum, chum?' and they would throw out chewing gum and chocolate, and sometimes they would throw us out part of their rations. We would scramble to catch them and would then run home with our prize if we were lucky. When I managed to catch one of the parcels, I eagerly gave it to my foster mother. When she opened it and saw the contents she remarked 'Just look at what they get, all our boys get is dog biscuits.' Instead of being pleased she was really annoyed.

I don't remember much about the first school I went to in those days except that it was a small school close to the church in West Hyde, about a mile away from where we lived in Maple Cross. Nobody owned a car in our road and there was no school bus, so all of the children had to walk to school in all weathers, often trudging through thick snow in the winter and walking back in the dark. Children were not mollycoddled back then and we thought nothing of it, we just accepted it. But even if life was harder it was much more fun. We hardly ever played indoors. All our games were in the street playing hopscotch, two ball, whip and top etc., or we would ride our bikes whizzing down the hills with one of us sitting on the crossbar (no helmets or knee pads) and we loved it. Sometimes we would go scrumping over the fields and disappear for hours and nobody was worried that we would come to harm. Obviously it was a different world then, but I think that although health and safety tries to protect children today, it has taken all the joy out of childhood.

Then the day came when I was walking home from school with some of the other children, and as we reached the houses, we heard a lot of cheering and shouting. People were hanging out of the windows screaming 'The war's over, the war's over!' Although I was only about ten years old then, I could sense the happiness and excitement. Very soon our street, like thousands of others all over Britain, had a street party. There were things brought out of the cupboards that people had saved from their rations and put by for Christmas, or a special day. Some of the parents of the evacuees brought black market things like butter, cheese, coffee and – most prized of all – tinned pineapple.

Soon after this, the parents of the other evacuees came to take their children back home to London, but my parents didn't come to collect me and my sister. We were not aware that my mother had divorced my father, remarried, become widowed and then married my father again. Because she had changed her name several times the authorities couldn't trace her, and I imagine she didn't want to be found. So my sister and I remained with our foster parents long after the other children had left, and we just assumed that we would live with them for ever.

Chapter 2

Mummy dearest

➤┤◆➤○➤◆┤◄

I was almost twelve years old when out of the blue, my mother arrived in a taxi and said we must go back with her. I was devastated, because I loved my foster parents and by now they were the only parents I knew. Within one day, my whole life changed. I was taken away from the happy and carefree life I had known to start a new life in a strange place with people who were practically strangers. We didn't go back to London like the other evacuees, but to Denham close to

Uxbridge, where my parents had brought a lovely bungalow with a large garden that ran down to the river. My father had suffered from TB for years and was advised to move out of London to a place where the air was purer.

I then discovered that I also had a younger brother who had been evacuated to live with a different family, and from the very beginning it was clear that he was the only child my mother had any feelings for. He could do no wrong in her eyes, while my sister and I were made to feel that we were a huge disappointment to her.

My sister began training to be a hairdresser in London and my brother and I started in new schools. Before we started, my mother went to see the headmaster to say she didn't want me to attend the religious instruction which was compulsory in all state-run schools at that time. This resulted in me finding out that I was 'different' from the other children. I soon learnt what anti-Semitism was, although I had no idea what being Jewish meant. I only knew that now I wasn't allowed to eat any of my favourite foods or go to church any more. In my teacher's eyes though, I was not only Jewish but I came from London, which she regarded as something to be ashamed of. I believe a lot of people thought at the time that most Londoners were gangsters and lived in the slums. I was made to feel I wasn't quite like the rest of the children.

I remember one day when the nurse came to the school to check if any of the children had lice, which was very common in those days, my name was immediately called out, and I had to sit in front of the class while my hair was checked, while the other kids chanted under their breath 'dirty Jew, dirty Jew'. I heard it and the teacher must have heard it, but the children weren't corrected. And if any child lost their pocket money or anything else, my desk would be searched, because I was the 'thieving little Jew'.

Most of the children in the school were nice

Christian children with fair hair and turned-up noses who had names like Brown, Smith and Jones, but when my name was called out at the morning roll call, I could hear the other kids sniggering. I hated my name, I hated having black hair and above all I hated being Jewish. I just wanted to be like them. I was unhappy at school and I was unhappy at home. I missed the life at Maple Cross; no more playing in the fields with my friends, or catching tiddlers in the stream, or climbing trees in the woods. Life now meant coming home after school and doing the housework, or preparing the vegetables for dinner. I wasn't allowed to go out or to have friends. I felt lonely and miserable and the days just dragged by. My only outlet was reading books, which enabled me to lose myself in another world. I wasn't allowed to read comics or the usual sort of magazines that teenage girls read; the only literature that my mother approved of was the classics or history, and although I originally had no choice in the matter, Greek Mythology and Egyptology became a love affair that has lasted all my life.

My mother was an exceptionally beautiful woman with flame-red hair and huge green eyes. She was tall and majestic and always wore black suits with a fox fur stole, high-heeled shoes and a hat with a veil, and smelt of heavy French perfume. She looked like a movie star, and everywhere she went people stared at her. I have never understood how she ended up with my father, as she was sophisticated, witty and charming and could speak several languages, whereas, my father, who came from the East End of London, was not at all attractive, had no interests other than fishing, and was weak and lazy. He worshipped my mother, but unfortunately for him the feeling was not reciprocated. He was completely under her thumb and seemed totally oblivious to how she treated my sister and me. I suppose, as they say, that love is blind.

But while my mother, the movie star, looked like a million dollars, I was sent to school without a winter coat, proper shoes or clean clothes and had only one pair of knickers, which I had to wash out each night to wear the next day. I was probably the poorest-dressed child in class (no social services in those days). If I ever complained that I needed new clothes her favourite reply was 'What for, who would look at you?' She never attempted to make me feel good about myself as most mothers would. Instead she would constantly criticize my appearance and make me feel that I was ugly. You never forget these kinds of remarks, especially when they come from your mother, and I think this is what gave me the low self-esteem that made me make such unfortunate choices later in life.

She was even more critical about my sister's appearance, but I suppose that was because my sister was very pretty and had her life before her, while my mother's looks were fading and she was trapped in an unhappy marriage. In all the time that my sister and I lived at home we never once received so much as a birthday card – it was as if we were nothing.

Although life was miserable for both my sister and me, my brother took advantage of being the favourite and would go out of his way to stir things up. He was particularly cruel to my sister and would make up lies about her just to get her into trouble, and of course my mother always believed him. I slept in the same room as my sister and looked forward to going to bed, because it was the only time we could talk to each other in private, and express our feelings. But one night, unbeknown to us, my brother was hiding under the bed. He then ran to my mother and told her an embellished version of our conversation, which made our relationship with her even worse.

Yet in spite of all my mother's failings and lack of any maternal warmth, I really loved her and wanted her to love me. People often assume that all women have a natural maternal instinct, but that isn't necessarily true. Not all women want to have children, and in the 1930s there wasn't a lot you could do if you became pregnant. My mother was an only child and had a very Victorian upbringing. As a baby she was cared for by a nanny and spent most of her childhood in an all-girls boarding school. She had never been part of a family, so had no idea of how to be a mother. I doubt if she was even aware that her attitude to us almost amounted to cruelty. Even though she didn't physically abuse us, she didn't need to – one of her withering looks was enough.

Because of the damage to his lungs caused by TB, my father spent a lot of time in hospital, and sadly, after a long and difficult operation, he developed a blood clot in his leg, which later had to be amputated. He had a tailoring business but could no longer travel to London, so he took in a partner who eventually cheated him, and the business ended up in the bankruptcy court, which made my mother despise him even more.

Before the war years she had enjoyed the high life. It was the time of the Roaring Twenties and the Jazz Age, and life must have been very exciting living in London then, especially for a beautiful woman. So moving to Denham, where nothing ever happened, and finding herself the sole breadwinner and supporting an invalid husband she couldn't stand, and three children she didn't really want, must have been absolute hell for her. Sadly, she was a woman who had so much potential, but never had the chance to fulfil her dreams. I imagine she was suffering from depression, but depression was not a thing people talked about in those days, or even considered an illness. Maybe if she had had the kind of treatment people are prescribed today she might have been different, although I very much doubt it.

We had been living in Denham for about two years when one Saturday morning my mother told us that a man would be coming in the afternoon with a baby monkey she had brought. My mother had no time for children but she loved animals, and we already had an Alsatian dog called Teddy, a ginger cat called Percy, a couple of guinea pigs and several budgerigars in an aviary, which, along with fishing, was my father's passion. My mother never said where she got the monkey from, but sure enough, in the afternoon a man arrived with a tiny little monkey wearing a red knitted dress, and he said her name was Lulu. He also brought a large wooden cage which was placed in an alcove in the kitchen. We all loved her and she became very spoilt, and before long she was the most important 'person' in the house. In the summer we would put her into a much larger cage outside, and when the weather was warm enough we would let her out to play in the trees, but it would take ages to entice her back, usually with a banana or some treats.

It wasn't long after we had her that it became very obvious that Lulu was actually a Lou, although we still carried on calling him Lulu and still referred to him as her. Once a year a garden fete was held in Denham village and some of the stars who had been filming at the nearby Denham Studios (now long gone) would attend. My mother suggested my sister and I should go and take Lulu with us. When we arrived, Petula Clark and several film stars were at the fete signing autographs, but more people were interested in Lulu than the stars, so for a short time she became a celebrity. The next week my sister and Lulu appeared in the local paper.

The area where we lived in Denham was called Willowbank. It was practically an island because it was surrounded on one side by the River Colne, with the Grand Union Canal running along the other side. A small weir formed where they both met and this became a huge attraction to fishermen, but only people with permits were allowed to fish on the river banks. Willowbank was a private area in the time that we lived there with only one entrance. All the properties were bungalows and there were strict restrictions on building extensions of any kind. On our front gate my mother had placed a placard that read 'Tradesmen Round the Back', as if we lived in a mansion. And although the majority of people who lived there were professional people, including an author, an artist and a scientist, my mother still considered herself to be superior to them and made no attempt to be sociable. They in turn referred to her as the 'Lady'.

Occasionally, I would have to go shopping with my mother in Uxbridge, which was mortifying, as she would stride past all the people who had been queuing for ages, march into the shop and bang on the counter and demand 'Get me so and so, my good man'. When we came out of the shop you could sense the anger and glares of the people still queuing. My mother was oblivious, but I would shuffle past them with my head down trying to avoid their eyes.

From the way she dressed, and with all her

airs and graces, my mother gave the appearance of being very wealthy, but in fact, she owed money everywhere. She was a chain smoker and couldn't do anything without having a cigarette first, so I was often sent out to buy fifty Churchman No. 1, her favourite brand. There would be a list of shops to avoid because she hadn't paid the bill, and there was always a pile of letters arriving in the post in different names that she used, because she couldn't get credit in her own name. I remember we had a tall green and cream cabinet in the kitchen; it was the first thing you saw when you walked through the door. The shelves were filled with expensive tinned food which could be seen through the glass panels, and they looked very impressive if visitors came, but the tins were empty and there was nothing behind them.

Despite the early anti-Semitic incidents at school I did eventually get accepted by the other kids and ended up loving my time there. I loved literature, history and maths, which I was very good at, so when I left school I got a job in an office training to be a bookkeeper. Going to work was a pleasure as the people were friendly and it was an escape from home. I didn't earn very much money, but as soon as I got paid I had to hand my wages over to my mother unopened, and she gave me back just enough to pay for my lunch and bus fare.

I was now allowed to go to the pictures once a week with one of the girls I worked with who my mother just about approved of, but I had to be home immediately after the picture ended. There were three picture houses in Uxbridge at that time, although most of the films were either westerns or musicals and they always seemed to feature Doris Day. Television was not yet available in most homes, so there was no other entertainment unless you had a gramophone, but of course my mother wouldn't have one in the house.

My sister wasn't allowed much more freedom than I was, even though she was almost twenty, although she was allowed to go to a Jewish youth club in Ealing once a week. It was there that she met and fell in love with a boy who was also a member of the club, and after their relationship became serious she told my parents that she wanted to marry him. My father as usual said nothing, but my mother was furious and there was a terrible row. However, she did reluctantly agree to meet him. When my sister brought him home I thought my parents would be pleased as he was well dressed and very polite, and he obviously adored my sister. He owned a dress shop in Walthamstow market, but of course that wasn't good enough for my mother. In her eyes he was no better than a barrow boy and she refused to even consider giving her consent. She forbade my sister to see him again, but for once my sister stood her ground, and after another huge row she left home in tears. Her name was never mentioned in the house again and I was forbidden to see her or even write to her. I was devastated as I had never been separated from her before.

She was my best friend and she had always protected me. I loved her and missed her dreadfully. Happily for my sister though, she did marry her boyfriend and was happily married for more than sixty years.

But for me life at home was now even more miserable. These should have been the happiest days of my life as rock & roll had finally reached Britain from America, and teenagers were buying records by Bill Haley, Buddy Holly and the Everly Brothers as well as Johnnie Ray and Dean Martin. The youth of Uxbridge would meet up in the Aero milk bar on Saturday nights before going to the dance hall above Burton's shop, where they would dance to the music of big bands, like Joe Loss and Ted Heath. But of course, this was out of bounds for me, so most of it passed me by. However, although there was more freedom for younger people in the late fifties and early sixties, there was also a very dark side to this period. Homosexuality was still considered to be a crime, and men who were accused of being homosexual were hounded out of their jobs and disgraced and some were even jailed. Hanging was still the punishment for murder which unfortunately resulted in two innocent men, Timothy Evans and Derek Bentley, being hung for crimes they didn't commit, which ultimately led to the abolishment of capital punishment in 1964.

One day at work my girlfriend said that a fair was coming to Uxbridge at the weekend and why don't we both go. I knew I wouldn't be allowed to go even though I was nearly twenty, so I told my mother I was going to the pictures. I had never been to a fair before and to me it was magical, the coloured lights, the music and amusements – I thought I was in fairyland. I wandered around taking everything in and suddenly realised I couldn't see my friend. I started to panic and ran around looking for her. Out of the corner of my eye I noticed a man had been following me, and I became really scared. It must have showed that I

was frightened because a tall blonde good-looking
boy came up to me and asked if I was with anyone.
I replied that I was with a friend but couldn't find
her, and he said 'Don't worry I will walk you
home'. When I got close to my home I said I would
walk the rest of the way by myself just in case my
brother was about, because unlike me he was
allowed to go out anywhere with no questions
asked. My knight in shining armour, whose name
was Richard, said he wanted to see me again, so I
told him where I worked, and before I could say
goodbye he kissed me goodnight. I know this
sounds unbelievable today, but at nineteen this
was the first time I had ever been kissed by a boy.
I went indoors in a dream. I had met my hero; I
was in love.

Chapter 3

Richard

I started to meet Richard secretly for the next couple of weeks, and although I felt guilty of lying to my mother I was convinced that he was worth it. He took me home to meet his family and they made a huge fuss of me, which felt marvellous. He had brothers and sisters and they seemed a really close family, and I wanted to be part of it.

When I got home you could cut the atmosphere with a knife. Apparently my brother found out that I had been seeing someone and he couldn't wait to tell my parents. My mother started screaming at me that I was a slut and a little tramp, egged on by my brother, who added accusations that he had made up just to make things worse. My father as usual agreed with my mother and said nothing when I was told to get out. I left home just like my sister, with nothing but the clothes on my back. I took the bus to my friend's house, as I didn't know where else to go. When I told her mother what had happened and she saw how distressed I was, she told me I could stay the night and made up the settee for me, but although it was warm and comfortable I couldn't sleep. My mind kept going over and over the enormity of what had just happened.

In the morning after breakfast my friend and I went to work together. Shortly afterwards the supervisor called me into her office and said she had heard what had happened and asked me what I was going to do. I started to explain and burst into tears. She told me not to get upset, and said that after work she would come with me to see my parents and try to sort things out. So when the office closed the supervisor and my friend came with me to my house. Although I had a key I was afraid to just walk in, so I knocked on the door, which was something I had never had to do before. My mother opened the door and before I could speak she said there was nothing to discuss, as I no longer lived there. I asked if I could take some of my clothes, and ignoring me she said to my supervisor 'Wait', and closed the door.

We stood there in the garden and I started to cry again, because in spite of everything I didn't want to leave home. After a while my mother opened the door and threw out some bags stuffed with my belongings. We picked them up and walked away. My friend's mother said I could stay there until I sorted myself out, so when I next saw Richard and told him what had happened, he said he would ask his parents if I could stay with them.

His parents welcomed me and said I could

share a room with one of his sisters. It felt strange, as I had only known him for a few weeks and almost immediately his parents were pushing us to get married. Before I knew what was happening it was all arranged, and less than three months after our first meeting we were married. I was still a virgin the first night we slept together, but instead of the loving words of endearment I had anticipated, his comment was 'Now you're just like any other old tart'.

The blinkers were off. Although I thought I was in love in the beginning, I think I was just in love with being in love. I would have married Quasimodo if he had said 'I love you'.

Soon after the wedding, we rented a couple of rooms in a house close to his family, and I carried on working at the office. My new husband didn't have a job, so I paid for everything, which was very difficult as I didn't earn very much. When I got paid my husband took my wages to pay for the rent and bills etc. I didn't think anything of it, as it was what I was used to. I was unaware at the time that the rent wasn't being paid, or anything else for that matter. I hardly ever saw him as he spent most of the time at his parents' house. In the evenings he went out, but he never asked me to join him, and he never came back until the early hours of the morning. When I asked him where he had been he would get really angry and say I was a nag, and that he wished he had never married me. Soon after, I found out that he was in a relationship with another girl, who he had been seeing for months before he met me, and that she was expecting his baby.

It was now obvious that the man I had thought of as my knight in shining armour was just a petty crook, a liar and a cheat, and his family had only pushed us to get married because they thought I was rich, after they found out where my parents lived. It was about this time that I discovered I was also pregnant. I worked as long as I could, but now there was almost no money coming in and my husband was hardly ever home.

I had been married for less than a year when my husband left me to live with his girlfriend. On top of all this, because the rent had not been paid I was given notice to leave. I felt sick with worry. The baby was due in a few weeks, I had very little money and very soon I would be homeless.

I needed to get some things from the chemist, so I went to Uxbridge, and afterwards with the little bit of money I had left in my purse I went to the milk bar to use their toilet. I didn't have enough money to buy anything to eat so I just sat there. I must have sat there for hours; the waitress kept looking at me, but she didn't say anything.

It was the era of the 'teddy boys' and they often used this café before going to the pub. While I sat there a group of them came in wearing their long jackets, drainpipe trousers, suede shoes and DA hairstyles, and before long they started arguing about which record to play in the juke box. I could see the waitress talking to them and they kept looking across at me, which made me feel uncomfortable. Then, after a while, one of them came over to where I was sitting, put some money on the table and said 'here love, get yourself something to eat'. I have never forgotten this gesture and it just goes to show that you should never judge by appearances. While the local papers were constantly branding them thugs and hooligans, here they were giving money to a pregnant woman they didn't even know.

I was still sitting there when the waitress started to close up. She came and sat next to me and said 'I'm sorry love, but I've got to close now, don't you have somewhere to go?' I started crying, and because I had no one else I could talk to, I told her everything. When I had finished she seemed very concerned and asked if I could come back early in the morning, as she knew someone who might be able to help me. I went back to the flat feeling a little relieved that I had talked about it and hoping that maybe everything would be all right after all.

The next day I met the waitress, whose name was Margaret, outside the milk bar and she said she knew of a woman who was high up in the Salvation Army who helped unmarried mothers and abused women, and that she lived not far from the café, so we could walk there. It didn't take us very long to reach the house, which was very large with a beautiful garden. We knocked on the door and a very well-dressed middle-aged woman opened the door and asked us what we wanted, although looking at me it must have been quite obvious. She didn't ask us inside, so we had to talk on the doorstep. After I explained my situation she didn't say anything at first, then looking me up and down she asked me what church I belonged to. Of course I had to say that I was Jewish. Her attitude then became quite frosty and she said 'You are married, and if you are not living with your husband you are not abused, so I can't help you'.

Margaret then became annoyed and added

'But her husband has left her and she's homeless and pregnant'. The woman replied, 'She should try the synagogue, their lot always stick together' and with that she closed the door.

Nowadays, although I give to many charities, whenever someone rattles the Salvation Army box in my face, I think of that day standing on the doorstep, desperate for help, and I still can't forgive them. Margaret apologised for the woman's attitude and said 'Don't let it upset you, come back to the café and have a hot drink'. I stayed there for a while but when it started filling up I left and went back to the flat.

I awoke the next morning with a sick feeling of hopelessness; I couldn't see any future and had never felt so frightened or alone. I decided to go and see the landlord to explain that my husband had left me, and that I didn't know the rent hadn't being paid. He was actually quite a decent man, and when he saw that I was heavily pregnant, he said I could stay until the baby was due, but I couldn't come back afterwards.

I was grateful for that at least. In the next couple of weeks I didn't go out much. I put the few belongings I had in boxes ready for when I would have to move, although I had no idea where I would move to.

That night when I went to bed I tried to sleep, but the stomach pain that had just been niggling earlier in the evening started to get much worse. I was sure my labour had started, but I didn't know what to do or who to call. I was scared and now in real pain, so I called an ambulance and was taken to Hillingdon Hospital. I had only attended the ante-natal classes towards the end of my pregnancy and really had no idea of what to expect.

On arrival, after my details were taken, I was shown to a cubicle and told to undress and put on a hospital gown. Then, after what seemed like hours, a nurse came in with a bowl and some instruments and said I would have to be shaved down below, which I found humiliating. I was then given an enema and taken to have a bath. When the pains got really unbearable I was wheeled down to the delivery room. I was now writhing in pain, and the nurse showed me a rubber mask and told me to breathe through it. The mask was similar to the mask the dentist used when taking a tooth out. It was supposed to make the pains easier, but it hardly made any difference to me.

I gave birth to a little girl in the early hours of the next day, the 9th of November 1956, and I called her Susan.

In the 1950s you had to stay in hospital for ten to fourteen days after giving birth and most of the other mothers were crying and begging to go home, but I didn't mind as I had no home to go to. While in the hospital I was shown how to wash my baby and how to change a nappy, and as I was unable to breast feed I was shown how to make up a bottle feed. Other than that I was allowed very little contact with my little daughter. Visiting times were a nightmare. The husbands would arrive with flowers and chocolates and spend the whole time hugging and kissing their wives, while the grandmothers went overboard with the new babies. It didn't take long before the nurses noticed that no husband or mother ever came to see me or my baby, and I was moved into the ward used mostly for unmarried mothers. In those days unmarried mothers were looked upon as being prostitutes and treated like dirt. Even the other mothers looked down on them as if they were inferior because they had got themselves 'into trouble', the term used for girls who became pregnant out of marriage.

When the time came for me to leave the hospital, I was told the matron wanted to see me and I was shown into her office. I sat down nervously but surprisingly she seemed quite nice. She asked me all about myself and what my plans were regarding my daughter. I told her the truth about my situation and after a pause she said 'look, you are not the first woman to be abandoned by their husband, and I can offer you a temporary solution'. I fidgeted on the chair waiting to see what she was going to suggest. 'There is a children's home not far from here that take in babies...'

I interrupted, 'I don't want my baby put in a home!'

'Just a minute, let me finish' she added. 'you have nowhere to live at the moment, let alone to take a baby to. I am offering you a chance to get on your feet, find a job and a decent place to live and then you can have your daughter back. So think about it, because the alternative could be much worse'.

I sat there in silence. I had heard about these homes where children were taken from their mothers and adopted against their will.

'Are you sure I can get my baby back if I can find a job and a place to live?' I asked.

'Yes, I wouldn't lie to you, but you will have to

get a job to pay towards the upkeep of your daughter. With regard to somewhere to live, there is a woman in Hillingdon who often takes in young girls and women like you. She doesn't charge very much in return for small jobs like shopping and cleaning. Are you interested?'

Of course I jumped at the chance. She wrote down her address and the address of the children's home and assured me that my daughter would be well looked after, and that I could visit her once a week. I left the hospital with just a piece of paper, but that little piece of paper would be the future for me and my daughter.

I knew the area in Long Lane where the woman lived and decided to go there straight away, as I had nowhere else to go. The house was a very small terraced house with just two up and two down with a tiny garden in the front. My hands were shaking as I knocked on the door and waited, not knowing what to expect. To my relief, when the door opened, an elderly woman with a kind face smiled at me and asked me in. She showed me into the front room which was full of furniture, pictures and knick-knacks, but lovely and cosy. She offered me a cup of tea and told me to make myself comfortable.

'My name is Mrs Whiting' she said. 'Now you tell me all about yourself'. So I told her everything; about my life with my parents and about my marriage and how I came to be homeless. She was very understanding, and said she had gone through a similar experience many years ago and that was why she tried to help girls like myself.

After we had talked for some time she said that the last girl had left several weeks ago, so if I wanted to I could move in straight away. I was delighted and couldn't believe my luck. It was the first time that someone had been really nice to me and not judged me. I followed her up the very steep stairs and she showed me the little box room which would be mine if I wanted it. I told her I would come back as soon as I had collected my belongings from the flat, but when I got there it had been emptied apart from my clothes. I returned the keys to the landlord and asked him what had happened to my things, and he told me my husband had taken them. There wasn't that much to take, but some of the personal items like photographs and letters had meant a lot to me. However, I collected my clothes and went back to Long Lane feeling optimistic that this was going to be a new start.

My room was very small with just a bed and a wardrobe, but it felt homely and Mrs Whiting was really kind. There was hardly any housework that needed doing and I think what she really wanted was the companionship. We got on really well and after a while she sort of adopted me, and became like the mother I had always wanted.

The following week I applied for a job at the chemists Timothy Whites & Taylors which was next to Uxbridge train station, and I was put on the make-up counter, which I loved. I was still not earning very much money, but at least I didn't have to give my wages to my husband or my mother any more, although I now had to pay rent, food, clothing and travel expenses. Also, a percentage of my wages went to the children's home for the upkeep of my daughter. I was allowed to visit her at weekends, which was heartbreaking because we had never had the chance to bond with each other, and when I tried to play with her she would keep running back to the nurses. Of course it was only natural, as they were the ones who fed her, bathed her and looked after her every day, but I felt a total failure as a mother.

One day after she had been in the home for over a year, I was visiting my daughter as usual when I was told that the supervisor wanted to speak to me. I sat in her office and was given a cup of tea while I waited. She came in, and sitting down behind her desk, took out a file which she glanced through quickly before looking at me.

'The board have decided it would be better for

your daughter if she was fostered with a family, as they feel she is becoming institutionalised' she said. I sat there numb, trying to work out what this would mean. The supervisor then added 'I see you're not happy about this decision. Are you in a position to take care of your daughter yourself?' she paused. 'You go to work don't you?' I nodded. 'So, who would look after Susan when you are working?' I sat there unable to answer. 'This is just a temporary arrangement which we feel would be better for your daughter. As you need time to think about this, I have asked a welfare woman to visit you where you are living, to explain the situation, and make sure you fully understand.' I got up and left her office feeling confused and apprehensive.

Chapter 4

Donald

In the meantime, I was happy working at Timothy Whites & Taylors. I got on well with the staff and customers and was chosen with three other girls to go to London to do a beauty course at the Helena Rubinstein Institute. Sometimes I would practise my new make-up skills on Mrs Whiting and her friends, and she made me feel that I was part of her family.

Although my divorce was not yet finalised, I started to date boys who also lived in Hillingdon.

They often started off keen, but the relationships didn't last long after they found out that I was married to a petty crook and had a child in a foster home. This was probably due to pressure from their mothers, who I suppose were only looking after their sons' interests, and I obviously wasn't considered good daughter-in-law material. Then one Saturday when I was out with a friend, I was introduced to Don, a friend of her boyfriend who had just finished in the Merchant Navy. He was not my type, but he appeared to be decent and honest and seemed very attracted to me. When he asked me out on a date, because of all my past experiences, I decided to tell him straight away about my husband and my daughter. He said he wasn't interested in what had happened in the past, he was only interested in who I was now.

So I started to go out with him and it very quickly became serious, although it wasn't yet a sexual relationship. In the meantime, the new arrangement for me seeing my daughter was that a welfare woman would bring her to Ruislip railway station and I would be allowed to spend an afternoon with her. This was very difficult, because there wasn't really anywhere I could take her in that time. Even worse, to her I was now a stranger. When I took her hand and tried to walk with her, she would keep trying to pull free and kick my legs, screaming 'I want my mummy, I want my mummy!' It became so upsetting that instead of looking forward to these meetings, I started to dread them.

Several months had gone by when one day, when I got home from work, Mrs Whiting told me there were two women waiting to see me. They said they had come to discuss my situation, and asked me if anything had changed in my circumstances. I told them that I was now seeing a man and that he wanted to marry me. 'How can that be my dear, you're still married to Susan's father, aren't you?' one of the women said in a condescending tone.

'I know, but I am going to get a divorce as soon as I can,' I replied. The other woman butted in 'Look, our main concern is for the welfare of your daughter. She is very happy where she is and her foster parents want to adopt her.'

There was a stunned silence while I tried to take it in. 'But she's my daughter!' I protested. I was now getting upset. 'They said it would only be temporary, until I could have her back.'

'Well how do you suppose you can do that? You are not yet divorced, you go to work, and you can't bring a baby up here. In any case, the authorities would never allow it.'

At this point Mrs Whiting came in with tea and biscuits, and gave me a pitying glance as she could see I was being bullied. Then the other woman came up with the usual patter. 'If you really love your daughter as you say you do, you would give her the best chance in life, which at the moment you can't offer her'. She quickly added, 'you are a young and healthy girl, I'm sure you will have more children when the time is right, but the couple who have Susan can't have children of their own and they really love her.' With that they stood up, preparing to leave. 'Think about it, because if you don't agree Susan could be made a Ward of Court'.

As soon as they left Mrs Whiting came over and hugged me. 'Don't take any notice of them love, they can't do that. Don't you be rushed into doing something you will regret later.'

But unfortunately, it didn't end there. The women returned several times, sometimes on their own and sometimes with a man. Each time they came they put more pressure on me, always repeating the mantra, 'if you really loved your daughter you would give her up'.

I had been living with Mrs Whiting for about eighteen months when Don said that there was a really nice caravan for sale on the site in Langley where his brother was living, and he wanted to buy it, and for me to move in with him. I was happy living in Long Lane, but I thought that if I moved in with Don I would then be able to get my daughter back. So although I was sad to say goodbye to Mrs Whiting, as I had grown very fond of her, I moved in with Don, feeling optimistic about the future.

To start with, life was quite pleasant living in Langley. The caravan site was in a cherry orchard which belonged to a family who also owned a farm shop, where we could buy milk and groceries. I carried on working at Timothy Whites & Taylors and Don was working at a subsidiary of the Ford Motor Company. I had started divorce proceedings against my husband, although I had no idea where he was, and thought I was now in a good position to fight for my daughter.

Then, several weeks before I was due to attend court, I found out that I was pregnant again. Don was thrilled about becoming a father, but he refused to accept Susan, and I felt betrayed. I now accepted that I had no choice but to agree to the adoption and reluctantly signed the papers. I carried on working until a few weeks before the baby was due, then on 5th November 1959, almost three years to the day after I had given birth to Susan, I gave birth to my second daughter, Alison.

When at last my divorce became finalised, Don and I decided to get married. And for the first couple of years I was quite happy. I loved the caravan, it was warm and cosy, and it was the first time I had a place I could actually call home.

It was during this time when I was shopping in Uxbridge one day that quite by accident, I bumped into my mother. She said 'Hello Carole' as if there had never been any bad feeling between us. I always knew that this might happen one day, and in spite of our past differences, I was really pleased to see her. We went to a nice little café for a cup of tea and sat and talked. I told her that I was married, and where I was living, and asked her to visit us sometime. She said that my brother was constantly demanding money and using threatening behaviour towards her and my father, and that they were afraid of him. I had to bite my tongue not to remind her how she had spoilt him, and to say that this was the way he was repaying her.

Don was now earning good money, and after living in the caravan for about three years, we had saved up enough to buy a small semi-detached house, also in Langley. So when my daughter was old enough to go to nursery school, I started a part-time job at a new clothing factory, Pasold's Ltd, which was close to Langley railway station. I didn't really like the job, but it was convenient. One of the girls who worked with me was called Ellen, and she told me that she was unhappy in her lodgings but had nowhere else to go. I knew what it was like to be homeless and I felt sorry for her, so I asked Don if she could move into our spare room. He was reluctant at first, but then said it could work out quite well as she could help around the house and possibly do a bit of babysitting. He was a member of the union and used to go to a lot of meetings in the evening, which wives were not allowed to attend, or at least that's what he told me. We hardly ever had sex any more and I suspected he was seeing other women.

Ellen and I got on really well, and having her there gave me more time to spend with my daughter. After losing Susan, I was terrified that I might also lose Alison, and I became so wrapped up in her that I didn't notice that my marriage was deteriorating. We were constantly arguing, and Don seemed to disagree with everything I said and did. I could never do anything right in his eyes; he used to say that I was a fabulous cook, but now the food was either overcooked, undercooked, too salty or not salty enough. He would even undermine the way I brought up Alison by encouraging her to do the opposite of what I had wanted: if I said she couldn't have something, he would say she could, if I put her to bed, he would pick her up and let her come out.

Not only that, he would often belittle me in front of friends and neighbours, and I started to really dislike him. He was friendly with the landlord of the Red Cow, a pub in West Drayton, and on occasion we would spend an evening with him and his wife, even though I don't drink myself. But I loved the atmosphere and I liked the wife, and became very friendly with her. I hated the job at Pasolds, so when she asked me if I would like to work in the pub two or three nights a week, I really wanted too, but I wasn't sure if Don would agree. I was surprised when he suggested that I could work there two nights a week while he looked after Alison, as long as the rest of the week was his.

I started work in the pub on a Wednesday night, because that was when it was usually very quiet. I was very nervous at first, especially when it came to adding up a round, because the tills were not computerised then. Often a crowd of workmen would come in and they would all drink something different, and I had to quickly add everything up in my head. It didn't take long before I got to know all the regulars and I really enjoyed all the banter and gossip. One of the regulars was an old man who only drank Guinness. He was fanatical about the colour and size of the froth on top, and if it wasn't quite right he wouldn't pay for it. And there were the old ladies who would sit in the corner making their gin & tonics last all evening. Some of the young girls would confide in me all their problems, or try to get me to fix them up with some boy that they fancied. I seemed much better at matchmaking for them than I was with my own life.

There were also several small-time crooks and gangsters who came in to play cards, and probably work out their next job! But they always treated me with respect and left me good tips. I remember one night when one of them came rushing up to the bar and said 'if the Old Bill come in Carole, I was here all night, OK?' but my favourite customers were the workmen and bricklayers who were working nearby. They were always funny and cheerful and good natured. Some of them would chat me up and tell me I was beautiful, which I put down to the beer talking, but one really good-looking guy called Barrie would lean on the bar staring at me for most of the evening. When I gave him his change he would squeeze my hand tightly and not let go until his friends called him over to play darts. I started to look forward to him coming in and made a special effort with my make-up and hair. Most of the other bar staff worked part time like me, but they weren't always reliable, so I often had to do extra shifts at short notice. Because I was a friend, the landlord trusted me and often left me in charge if he and his wife wanted a night off.

I couldn't stop thinking about Barrie, and even when I wasn't working at the pub I was always thinking about him. I realised that I was falling in love with him, but at that time I didn't have any intentions of taking it further. On the nights I didn't work I tried to encourage Ellen to go out and have fun, but she said she preferred to stay in with me. She never talked about her family and didn't seem to have anybody in her life, so I went out of my way to make her feel part of my family. She didn't seem to like Don very much and always took my side when we had a row. She was always telling me that it wasn't true that there were union meetings several times a week, or that wives weren't allowed to go to the socials. I always denied this, although I knew she was right, but by now I didn't really care, and I confided in her my feelings for Barrie.

All I could think of was going to work and seeing him. When I first met him I wasn't aware that he was married, and to start with it was just an innocent bit of flirting, but as my feelings for him grew stronger I started to feel guilty, although I had never actually done anything wrong.

It would possibly never have gone further than that if Don hadn't forced my hand. It all came to a head one night when the landlord said he couldn't run me home. He asked the guys who had been playing darts if one of them would take me home and to my delight, Barrie said he would. I got into the old Cadillac he was so proud of and it was the first time I had been alone with him.

When we reached my house he leaned over to kiss me goodnight. As I got out of the car I noticed that Don had come home early, and he had been watching me through the window. Before I could even get through the front door I could see he was shaking with anger. He pushed me against the wall and started hitting me. I tried to explain that it was only a lift home, but he was beside himself. 'I think I'm falling in love with Barrie!' he sneered, thumping me up against the wall again. I realised that the girl I had felt sorry for and taken in and treated as family was a 'cuckoo in the nest' and had betrayed my confidence to someone she professed not to even like. I could hear Alison crying and tried to get up the stairs to see her, but Don pulled me away, dragging me by the hair, and pushed me out of the door.

My mother, Irene Josie Gabriela Musgrave-Wood,
who died 25th September 1981

My father, Nathan Mitzman, who died
25th September 1983

Me as a little girl

Me just before I emigrated to Israel

At my desk in the Sahar Insurance office

With my beloved Poppy

My first grandchildren as babies: Paul, Sarah, Dawn

My second grandchildren as babies: Natalie, Kerry, David

My daughter Alison

Chapter 5

Barrie

Once again I was out in the cold with nowhere to go, but this time it was so much worse because I knew I was to blame, and I was hurting my daughter, which I had never meant to do. Even though I was no longer happy in my marriage, I would never have walked out and left my daughter, or my home. I rang my friend Bobby, who had been our neighbour when we lived in the caravan. She had won some money on the football pools and was now living in a beautiful bungalow in Wraysbury. Bobby and her husband often came to dinner with Don and me and we also spent a lot of time with them. I couldn't think who else to call as it was late in the evening, and I thought it would only be for one night.

I waited in the road until her car pulled up, and on the way to her place, I told her what had happened. The next day I went back to my house thinking that after Don had cooled down it would be all right. Ellen opened the door and looked at me as if I was a stranger. I went to step inside, but she pulled the door and tried to shut it. I grabbed hold of the door and again tried to get inside, but she had put the safety chain on.

I couldn't believe that this supposedly timid person that I had taken pity on, and given a home to, was refusing to let me into my own house. I was desperate to see my daughter but realised I was up against a brick wall, so I went to the pub to tell them I couldn't work there any more as I didn't know where I would be staying. As I left the pub I saw Barrie drawing up in the car park in his old Cadillac. I told him what had happened and he said he would come round and see me at Wraysbury if Bobby and her husband didn't mind. Actually, Bobby and Les were a very laid-back couple. They had what is now called an 'open marriage', and when they met Barrie they really liked him – in fact everybody who met Barrie liked him. Bobby said I could stay until I had sorted myself out and then decided that she would go and see Don about allowing me to see Alison. This was a clever move on her part, because she knew how much Don liked her and trusted her judgement.

It was decided that because Alison was happy in her school and had friends in Langley she should stay with her father, and this was decided without going to court. In the meantime I couldn't sponge off Bobby, so I needed to get another job. There was a lovely old pub in Wraysbury, very close to the bungalow, so I applied for a job there.

With my experience as a barmaid I was taken on straight away. I started just working at lunchtimes but very soon I was working evenings as well.

The customers who used this pub were very different from the customers I was used to at the Red Cow. Mostly they were businessmen and company directors and I got many chances to go on dates. Barrie started using the pub in the evenings when I was working, and he became very jealous when some of the guys would chat me up. He made it very obvious that we were a couple and because he was built like a heavyweight boxer, nobody challenged him.

While I was living in Wraysbury I was able to see my daughter every other weekend as well as some weekdays, if and when it suited Don. I didn't usually see him on these occasions, so I had the humiliating ordeal of having to arrange it through Ellen, who was now firmly ensconced in my house. It was made clear that I couldn't have my daughter if Barrie was with me, which I could understand, but it meant that I had to take two buses each way and very often it would be pouring with rain. Ellen delighted in telling me I could pick Alison up at a certain time and then leave me waiting outside in the street, sometimes for more than an hour, or say it wasn't convenient to see her today so I should come back tomorrow. But eventually visiting my daughter became easier because Don had started a new relationship and Ellen wanted more time off, so it suited them.

I can't say that Don and I ever got back on friendly terms, but we were at least civil to each other, and he stopped insisting that Alison couldn't meet Barrie – he even allowed us to take Alison on holiday with us several times. We took her to the Isle of Wight, which she really loved, and on another occasion we took her to Majorca, which I think is the only time she has ever been abroad.

Barrie had now separated from his wife, and I felt very guilty about it as I was sure it was because of me, and I didn't want anyone else to get hurt. He said he was thinking of renting a flat in Slough which would be easy for him to get to work (he was a building contractor, in partnership with his cousin), and asked me to move in with him. I was over the moon, as by now I was crazily in love with him. It was a furnished flat on the ground floor in Upton Court Road, and when we moved in it felt like all my dreams had come true.

We soon made friends with a couple who lived in a similar flat next door. The woman was called Sheila and she got me a job in her office at Calor Gas in the accounts department. I was earning reasonably good money, but although Barrie's income was much higher than mine, he had to pay a huge amount of his wages to support his wife and children. We lived in the Slough flat for about three years and were very happy, but for Barrie the flat was too small – he wanted to own his own house

When I received the divorce papers from Don I went to see a solicitor to ask him to represent my

THE GIRL ON THE STATION

interests. I didn't fight the adultery charge as it was true, but I insisted that my share of the house be held in my daughter's name, to give her some security later in life.

Several months later Barrie's wife also divorced him, so we were now free to marry. Our marriage wasn't exactly romantic; I just popped out of work to the registry office in my lunch break – but it was the happiest day of my life. Third time lucky, I thought! Even my parents accepted Barrie. He totally charmed my mother, which really surprised me, and he won my father over by talking about fishing. I think they would rather have had him as their son than me as their daughter.

I was now seeing much more of Alison, and I was alarmed at how much weight she had put on. She was fifteen and not yet finished school, but was in a relationship with a boy who was quite a lot older than her. I told Don that I was concerned, but he said it was none of my business. So when

Alison told me she wanted to get married on her sixteenth birthday, I was totally against it. I didn't realise at the time that she was pregnant, and even if I was I would still have been against it. She was still only a child and had had no experience of life. Needless to say, her father gave his permission, so there was nothing I could do.

Barrie and I were now much better off financially and we were soon able to buy a small semi-detached house at Cippenham, near the railway station. With Barrie being in the building trade he was able to make a lot of improvements to the house, adding an extension and putting in a spiral staircase and stained-glass windows etc, so it was the envy of the street. Neighbours were soon asking him to do alterations for them also.

I had never been so happy. I was married to the man of my dreams, and I couldn't believe my luck. He was nearly seven years younger than me, tall and really handsome. I saw how other women looked at him, but it was he who was always jealous of me. He would fly into a rage if a man smiled at me when we were out together, and he would accuse me of flirting if I so much as glanced at another man. I should have seen the warning signs, but I was so besotted with him that even when the accusations turned to violence, I convinced myself that it was because he loved me so much. Afterwards, he would cry and beg my forgiveness and swear it would never happen again, and we would end up making love. Then the next day he would buy me something beautiful like perfume or jewellery and everything would be wonderful again – until the next time.

Because he was in the building trade, a lot of Barrie's business deals were done in the pub. This meant that what started off as an occasional hour during the lunch break escalated to several hours every day. He also started going to the working men's club in the evenings, supposedly on business, and was drinking more and more heavily. Sundays were particularly bad for me, as after spending the whole morning preparing Sunday lunch, which he used to love, he wouldn't arrive home until well after the pub had closed, and then fall asleep on the settee, so the food was ruined. It seemed that my life was now built around the pub's hours, but I knew better than to criticize him when he had been drinking. I used to enjoy going to the pub with him on Friday nights because many of my friends would be there, but I was afraid to talk to any of their husbands in case I was accused of flirting again. Even though I only drank orange juice myself, I felt more and more uneasy as I watched Barrie knocking back pint after pint, knowing that he would then drive the car while he was well over the limit. His favourite comment was 'I drive better when I'm drunk than most people drive sober'. Although he had often lashed out in jealous rages when we were first together, he now lost his temper over the slightest thing, often grabbing me by the throat and pinning me up against the wall. And instead of begging my forgiveness as he used to do, he now said that I had driven him to do it. But I always forgave him, just as long as he told me he loved me afterwards.

One evening he came home with an old Jaguar car he had bought from a company director he had been doing a job for. I thought he had bought it for himself, but he said it was for me. I had never driven a car and had never really wanted to, but he said it would make it much easier for me to visit Alison when he couldn't take me. He gave me a few lessons when he had the time, but he shouted at me every time I made a mistake, which made me really nervous. So I booked twenty lessons with a professional driving instructor who put me at ease and made it feel easy. When I finished the course the instructor decided I was ready to take the test, although Barrie disagreed. Of course I never expected to pass, so I couldn't believe it when I was told I had passed, especially when I had made a mistake backing round a corner.

I was now legally able to drive on my own, but I was afraid to go very far. So on occasion I would pick up Sheila and drive to Burnham or Taplow to build up my confidence. I was now able to see more of Alison and even to visit my parents. I felt I was now in a good place. I was married to the man I loved and I had my own house and a fabulous car, so when the new law came out allowing adopted children to see their birth certificate when they reached the age of eighteen, I wrote to the Adoption Contact Register saying I had no objections to being contacted. For the first few months every time the phone rang I expected it to be Susan, but months turned into years and I never received that call.

However, I did receive a call from my mother. She said she was selling the bungalow and moving to the Isle of Wight to get away from my brother, who was making their lives a misery. She said she was going across on the ferry by herself but my father wasn't able to, so she asked if Barrie could possibly take him. I felt very sad to think that they were selling the bungalow, but of course it was their decision to make. We did drive my father down the following month, and although they had bought another bungalow it was nowhere near as nice as the one in Denham and the garden was much smaller.

I had been trying for years to trace where my sister was living in London. I knew what her married name was and after ringing hundreds of people in the phone book, I finally managed to trace her. Barrie drove me to where she lived the following week as I didn't have the confidence to drive in London, and when she opened the door I knew her immediately, although she didn't recognise me at first. It was a very emotional meeting; we sat for hours catching up on each other's lives. Of course I had fleetingly met her husband years before, during that fateful confrontation with my mother, so it was lovely to now meet him properly and to meet their two daughters. When I left, I kissed my sister goodbye and we promised never to lose touch again.

On the way home I couldn't help thinking how differently our lives had turned out. Whereas my sister was still married to the same man and living in a huge house in a wealthy area of London. I was on my third husband and living in a tiny house in Cippenham.

One evening when Barrie came home from a job he had been doing in Maidenhead, he said he had been working next to a synagogue, and asked me if I wanted to go and see it. I thought about it for days, because even though I was Jewish by birth it had never occurred to me to go to a synagogue. I knew almost nothing about my religion and wasn't really that interested in finding out. When I lived with my parents I knew there were certain things I couldn't eat, but apart from my mother lighting candles on Friday nights, the religious side was hardly ever discussed, at least not in front of me. So to this day I don't know why I decided to drive to Maidenhead one Sunday afternoon to see if I could find the synagogue that Barrie had mentioned.

I drove around for about half an hour before I found it and drew up outside. I was expecting to see an impressive building similar to a church, but was shocked to see that it was just an old house that had been converted.

After I had been sitting there for a while, an old man came out. He was about to walk away when he spotted me. He came over and asked if there was anything I wanted. I didn't know what to say, so I replied that I was just curious.

'Would you like to come in?' he asked. 'I would be happy to show you around'.

I hesitated and then thought, 'why not now that I'm here?' So I got out of the car and followed him inside. There were several chairs lined up against the wall and a small table piled up with books. He opened a door which had a Star of David on it and beckoned for me to join him. There were rows of chairs laid out like a classroom and I assumed that this was where the worshippers sat.

'Are you Jewish?' he asked. He seemed such a warm and kind old man that I was soon telling him my life story. I explained that I was Jewish by birth but knew absolutely nothing about the Jewish religion.

'Do you want to?' he asked.

'I don't really know' I said, which must have sounded stupid.

'Well why don't you come along one Friday evening and talk to the Rabbi? He would make you very welcome and would be happy to answer any of your questions.' I said I would think about it and left.

I thought about it a lot during the following week and the next Friday I drove back to Maidenhead and again sat outside the synagogue, trying to pluck up courage to go inside. This time there were quite a lot of people hanging about outside talking. There were several men wearing 'kippahs' (skullcaps) and several women, also some children. They were all gathered around the old man, who appeared to be of some importance to the group. Glancing across he noticed me sitting there, and recognising my car, he came over. 'I'm glad you decided to come back,' he said. 'Do come inside I will introduce you to the Rabbi'. Again I hesitated. 'Please come, the service will be starting shortly'.

For the second time I followed the old man inside. Pushing through the people crowded inside I was told to wait a minute while the old man went to find the Rabbi. He returned almost immediately with a nice-looking young man with a beard, wearing a skullcap and prayer shawl, though other than that he looked just like any other man of his age. He smiled broadly and shook my hand and suggested I stay for the service, then if I was still interested, he would speak to me afterwards and answer any questions I might have.

I settled into a seat right at the back and watched what everybody did. When they stood up, I stood up, and when they sat down, I sat down. The service was read in English, but most of the accompanying songs were in Hebrew. I didn't understand them, but I found the melodies moving and beautiful. When the service ended everybody shook hands with each other and stood around chatting. Several women came over to me and said they hoped I would be joining the congregation. Then refreshments and cakes some of the members had baked were brought in.

As the people started to leave, the Rabbi came over to me and introduced himself formally. He was a charming and charismatic man, very different from the stereotype I had imagined. He asked if I would like to discuss anything I didn't understand.

There were many things I didn't understand, but to start with, I asked him what was the difference between Orthodox and Reform Judaism. He replied, 'There are many differences.

For a start, an Orthodox Rabbi couldn't shake a woman's hand as I shook yours. And you wouldn't be able to drive to an Orthodox synagogue, as driving on the Sabbath is forbidden. There is also a very strict dress code in Orthodox Judaism, whereas Reform Judaism is much more relaxed'. He then said, 'If you are really interested in learning more, I will lend you a couple of books, and hopefully you will come back and join us'.

I took the books and thanked him. On the way home, the melodies sung by the congregation kept turning over and over in my head. I couldn't believe how much I had enjoyed the experience and I couldn't wait to go back.

When I got in, Barrie had not yet returned from the pub. When he did come in I could see he was in a good mood, so I told him all about it. I was surprised that he didn't put up any objections to my going somewhere without him, as he usually did. During the week I read as much as I could and found it really interesting. This was what my mother should have been teaching us, instead of just saying 'you can't do this' or 'you can't do that' without any explanation. Barrie still worked hard and drank hard, but he was now into fishing, and sometimes he would go on weekend fishing trips with his mates. I couldn't bear it when he was away – I could put up with almost anything as long as he came home at night.

Our Friday night routine now was me going to the synagogue and Barrie going to the pub. Some of the members of the synagogue only came on the High Holidays or if their son was due to be Bar Mitzvahed. I never missed a Friday and soon became one of the regulars. I was invited to quite a few functions and Barrie was also invited, but he never wanted to go. I was now a fully-fledged member and my name was in the book along with the Cohens, Levys and Goldbergs. It seems ironic that as a child my name branded me as being different, too Jewish, and now at the synagogue my married name of McGuire was too Christian.

I had been with Barrie for almost twelve years and our lives were going in different directions, but I was still madly in love with him. A friend of mine from the synagogue had managed to get tickets for a Frank Sinatra concert and asked if I would like to go with her. I was thrilled, because I knew it was a chance in a lifetime to see Sinatra live. I told Barrie I wouldn't be back till late and he was all right about it. However, I got home much later than I thought and I was worried that Barrie would kick off, but when I got in the house was empty. I didn't go straight to bed and made myself a cup of tea and waited for Barrie, as I was worried that he might have been involved in a car accident.

However, when he did come home about half an hour later, he was angry when he saw me, and accused me of checking up on him. I asked him where he had been and he turned on me and snarled 'Don't start. If you know what's good for you, you'll shut up'.

I went up to bed, as I sensed it wouldn't take

much for him to lash out. When he came up to bed I put my arm around him for a cuddle, as I wanted to be close to him and for him to say he was sorry. But he threw my arm off and turned over and went to sleep. I lay awake most of the night and didn't get to sleep until the early hours of the morning. When I woke up I had a dreadful headache and Barrie had already gone out.

One afternoon, I was making myself a cup of tea when Bobby rang to invite Barrie and me to dinner, because she would soon be leaving for Dubai. Her husband had signed a three-year business contract and was already working out there. When Barrie came home from work I told him Bobby had invited us to dinner, but he said didn't want to go as there was a film he wanted to watch, so I went by myself. Bobby told me she was worried because she wanted to let the bungalow for the time they were away, but so far she had not found anybody who she considered reliable enough to take care of it.

When I came back and told Barrie about it, he said, 'Why don't you stay with her for a few days? It may be years before you see her again'. I didn't really want to go, but I thought being away for a couple of days might be good for our marriage. After all, don't they say absence makes the heart grow fonder?

I was going to drive myself there, but Barrie said he needed to give the car an overhaul and this would be the perfect time. Silly, trusting, me! I didn't know that when Barrie gave me the Jaguar and said it was my car, it was in fact registered in his name.

I helped Bobby pack up her things, and then we had dinner with her mother, who lived next door. Bobby was flying out the next day, so I rang Barrie to ask him to pick me up in the morning. He was silent for a moment, then said 'Don't bother to come back'.

I wasn't sure I had heard right. 'What do you mean, don't bother to come back?' I asked him again. Again silence.

'My girlfriend is moving in with me' he said.

I couldn't believe what I was hearing. 'What girlfriend, what are you talking about, how can you move her into my house?'

'My house' he corrected me. 'I've paid much more money into it than you have, and I've done all the alterations.'

'But it's still half my house, by law' I insisted. With that he put the phone down.

I was stunned. How could this be happening to me again? What had I done wrong? I admit I was partly to blame for my marriage to Don breaking up, but I had never stopped showing Barrie how much I loved him. Perhaps that was the trouble. Did I love him too much? Had I smothered him with love?

I burst into tears. I couldn't stop shaking and I felt sick in my stomach. Bobby came back into the room. 'Whatever's the matter?' she asked, seeing how agitated I was. I tried to tell her, but I was so distraught I could hardly get the words out. But all Bobby could say was 'I'm not that surprised Carole. After all he left his wife and kids without a second thought, he's obviously got no conscience.'

I tried to make excuses for him. But thinking about my car, it now seemed as if he had planned this. I knew he could be violent, although he could also be very loving and generous. I certainly never thought of him as being manipulative.

Bobby had known me for years, so she suggested that I stay in the bungalow rent free while I sorted my life out, and when I wanted to leave, I could hand the keys over to her mother. She said it would be a favour to her as she knew I would look after the place, and I could keep an eye on her mother. She said she had been worried about what to do about the cat, but she knew it would be fine left with me. If it hadn't been for the circumstances I would have been thrilled to stay in her beautiful bungalow rent free. It was much bigger than my parent's old bungalow and the garden was huge, it even had a swimming pool.

That night, after Bobby had left, I walked around the bungalow. I had never felt so alone, and so afraid for the future.

Chapter 6

Finding my roots

➤━┥◆➤━O━◆➤┥━◄

I went back to working at the pub in Wraysbury for a while, and then one of the customers who worked at a small wrought iron business next to the pub told me his boss needed someone to answer the phone and do the accounts, and suggested I apply for the job. He said the man's name was Frank. So after I had finished my shift in the pub I walked round to the yard next door. The office was just a little shack on the side of the main workshop and it looked as if there were four or five men working there.

I was just wondering whether I should go in or not when a truck drove up and a huge man with hands the size of bunches of bananas got out and walked towards the 'office'. He was the image of Robert Mitchum, and not the kind of man you would pick a fight with.

'I see you've found the place then' he commented. 'You better come in.' Obviously this was Frank. Looking around quickly, I saw that it was a complete shambles, dirty mugs everywhere, piled up invoices all over the desk in no kind of order, and the telephone was filthy and there was rubbish everywhere. The other desk, which I assumed belonged to Frank, who owned the company, was even worse, with several smouldering cigarettes lying on top of books and more invoices. It was a wonder the place hadn't gone up in flames.

Frank noticed my expression and said, 'Don't worry darling, I'm sure you will soon get the place spick and span'.

Bloody cheek, I thought. He was obviously not aware of women's rights or sexism in the workplace.

Yet in spite of Frank's slightly chauvinistic attitude, I really liked him. He was honest and down to earth, and you knew where you stood with him, so I agreed to start the following week. As he had predicted, I did soon get the place spick and span, but only because I couldn't work in a disorganised and filthy area. I managed to sort out the invoices, putting them in date order and marking them either paid or unpaid.

I asked Frank why so many of the firm's invoices had not been paid. 'I've never had the time to send them' he replied. 'That's why I've got you'.

I started to make phone calls to the companies on the unpaid list, and I did manage to get some of the money in. But that was another problem, as Frank had no idea how to do any form of book keeping. I couldn't imagine how he had managed to put in his VAT and tax returns. He was thrilled with the work I had done so far and kept telling the guys in the yard that I was a genius.

One afternoon he asked me if I would go to a company in Hayes to get an order released that they had withheld, because Frank had not paid their bill. 'I haven't got a car, Frank' I said. 'You have now' he replied, throwing a set of keys on my desk. 'It's the little Mini and it's yours as long as you work for me.'

I drove to the company in the little Mini. I couldn't help comparing it to 'my' wonderful Jaguar, but at least it got me there. I explained that I had just started working for Frank, apologized for the oversight of the unpaid invoice and assured him it wouldn't happen again, and he released the order. Frank was delighted and insisted on taking me out to dinner in a smart restaurant in London. The guys in the yard were soon convinced I was having an affair with him, and he made it quite clear he would like to, but I was still very much in love with Barrie and hadn't given up on getting back with him. However, I was getting very fond of Frank. It was hard not to, as he was generous, kind and very funny. When I told him about Barrie, he banged his huge fist on the desk and said, 'Let me talk to him'. I knew what he meant by 'talk' and begged him not to get involved. 'You're a fool, Carole' he replied. 'That bastard will cheat you out of everything.'

I was now starting to enjoy living in Wraysbury. The bungalow was beautiful and in a lovely area. I got on really well with Bobby's mum and often took her shopping in the little Mini. I was happy working for Frank, as I could more or less do what I liked. When the grass needed cutting at the bungalow, Frank would send one of the guys in the yard to cut it for me. Life was beginning to look good.

Bobby's mum advised me to go to a solicitor to sort out my rights with regard to the house and maintenance. Frank gave me the number of a solicitor he had used in the past and said he would pay for it. When the papers had been served on Barrie, he rang me up and threatened me, and said that if I continued, he would come round and smash up Bobby's flat. He finished with, 'Don't mess with me or you'll be sorry'. I couldn't believe that this was the man who had professed to love me for ever. I told the solicitor I wasn't going to fight for the house or maintenance, and he told me I was tying his arms behind his back, making it impossible for him to get what I was entitled to.

In the meantime I was still regularly going to the synagogue. I decided I didn't want to be Jewish for just one evening a week, I needed to know who I really was, so I booked a holiday to go to Israel and Bobby's mum said she would cover for me at the office. Frank drove me to Heathrow and I flew to Israel by El Al. The heat hit me as soon as I got off the plane, and although I knew it would be hot, I wasn't expecting the humidity, which made my hair stick to my head and my clothes cling to my body, it was very uncomfortable. I had no idea how modern and noisy Tel Aviv was, but it was also very exciting.

When I reached the hotel, the receptionist advised me to book with a tour guide who would show me the best parts of the country. She said that one of the guides they used was called Avi and people who had used him spoke very highly of him. So that's what I did. Then came the shock: 'You will need to be down at the foyer at seven thirty a.m., so I will book your breakfast for seven a.m., all right?' I had trouble getting up at eight thirty in the morning, so I was terrified I would oversleep.

At six thirty in the morning the phone rang, and I was still half asleep. 'Your early morning call' the voice said. I scrambled out of bed and got washed and dressed and did my make-up. I went downstairs to where breakfast was laid out and was feeling very self-conscious. I was shown to a small table and asked what I would like to drink.

I asked for orange juice and was told I could have toast, eggs or cereal and afterwards to help myself from the buffet. I had never seen so much food in the morning.

When I had had enough to eat I went to the lobby and noticed a gorgeous-looking young man with long, curly black hair, leaning on the counter and talking to the receptionist. She must have told him it was me who was hiring him, because he strode over to meet me with his hand outstretched. '*Boker tov* (good morning), beautiful lady' he said. I would have been flattered, but I guessed this was his standard opening gambit.

He led me out to a large car and asked if I preferred sitting in the front or back. Of course I said the front. As I settled in he asked if there was any particular place that I wanted to see. I said I would like to see the places associated with the Old Testament and with Israel's ancient history. 'Right, so leave it up to me, I think I know the places that will interest you,' he said. With that we drove away and my tour of Israel began.

During the week that I was on holiday, we visited Masada, the fortress built by King Herod and used today for the initiation ceremony of Israel's young soldiers. We visited Jerusalem, which was absolutely stunning, spent time in the old Arab bazaar and went to the museum which held the Dead Sea Scrolls. We also went to Bethlehem, Nazareth and Caesarea, and in the evenings he sometimes came with me to eat in Tel Aviv, where the variety and choice of food was amazing. But sadly the week went by too fast and it was nearly time to leave.

I told Avi how impressed I was with the country and how I wished I could stay in Israel for ever. He said 'Why don't you? It's actually quite easy if you are Jewish, and you get a lot of help as a new immigrant. You should look it up when you return home.'

Frank met me at the airport and drove me to the bungalow, where I unpacked my things and opened the post that had piled up. I had only been back for about an hour when Bobby's mum knocked on the window. I let her in and gave her the present I had brought for her. She then told me that one of Bobby's son's had contracted a virus and was not responding to treatment, so she was coming back with the children. I was sorry for Bobby's son, but my first thought was 'Oh God, I've got to look for another place to live again'.

Bobby's mum must have guessed what I was thinking and she said 'I would be happy for you to live with me, Carole, but Bobby has a lot of arrangements to make so she won't be back until three or four weeks' time.'

I went back to work the following day only to find a similar mess to the one I had found the first day I started. Invoices on the floor and dirty mugs everywhere. After I had tidied up, I went to see the boys in the yard, and they seemed really pleased to see me.

'Poor old Frank has really missed you' one of

the boys said.

'Yes, I can see that from the mess in the office' I replied.

Very soon I was back into my usual routine, but it now became difficult working next to Frank, because he made it obvious that he wanted our relationship to be more than boss and secretary. Although he was very good to me and I liked his company, I didn't want to take it further than just good friends. I was not yet divorced from Barrie and my solicitor was still trying to get me the best deal he could.

The next Friday when I went to the synagogue I discussed my holiday in Israel, and told them I was thinking of going there to live. I was given a lot of advice for and against, but although I had thought about it, I hadn't really intended to do it. Meanwhile I couldn't see that my life was going anywhere. I was quite happy living with Bobby's mother, but knew it wasn't a permanent arrangement, and the office job was starting to get boring. I felt I needed a change.

On a whim I contacted the Jewish Agency in London and made an appointment to go to see them. But firstly I had to obtain my birth certificate, my parents' wedding certificate and most important, my divorce papers, which I hadn't got as I wasn't yet divorced. I had been reluctant to divorce Barrie as I stupidly believed that he still loved me, and we might get back together again. I realised that that ship had sailed when a neighbour informed me that he now had a baby with his girlfriend. This really hurt me, because I had desperately wanted a child with Barrie, but he had refused, saying he already had children and didn't want any more. So my solicitor now went ahead with the divorce on the grounds of adultery. He also advised me that although I had said I wasn't claiming for my half of the house, or maintenance, I should do so, as that would give him leverage to obtain a financial settlement.

To my surprise the divorce went through

quickly without any problems, but getting any money out of Barrie was proving much trickier. As expected, he started threatening me on the phone, until my solicitor sent him a warning letter. Eventually he agreed to pay me £10,000 if I dropped my claim for maintenance and half the house. My solicitor advised against it, but I wanted things finalised as soon as possible and accepted his offer.

I now had all the documentation that I needed and went ahead to apply for immigration to Israel (Aliyah). When the paperwork and plane ticket came through several months later, Frank couldn't believe it. He was terribly upset and said that I was selfish and didn't care who I hurt. I suppose in a way I was selfish, but I knew I couldn't live with Bobby's mum for ever, and I didn't want to end up marrying another abusive man, or becoming Frank's mistress.

Alison now had two children and her life was settled, so I felt this was a good time to go. Then an extraordinary thing happened. I was making coffee for Frank and the boys in the yard when the phone rang. Geoff, one of the guys answered it and handed the phone to me saying 'it's for you'. It was a young woman's voice. I said 'hello, who is this?' and the voice said 'Susan, your daughter'.

I started to shake all over, it was such a shock. When I was with Barrie I had expected this call, but it had never come. Now that it had, I didn't know what to say. I didn't want the others to see how shaken I was and tried to compose myself. I asked Susan if we could meet somewhere so we could talk, and she said she would be happy to meet me anywhere, so I asked if she knew where the Ostrich pub in Colnebrook was. She said she would find it and we agreed to meet the following Saturday, at eight in the evening.

When Frank looked at me he could see that I was shaken up, so I told him the whole story of Susan, which I had never told anyone, not even Alison. He said he would come with me to support me, but I insisted that this was something I had to do by myself.

The following Saturday I sat in the car park of the Ostrich in my little Mini, trying to pluck up courage to go in. I knew that Susan was probably feeling as nervous as me and I wondered how I was going to recognise her. I was just about to get out of the car when a car pulled up and parked close by. As I watched, a tall, attractive, well-dressed young woman around twenty years old got out of the car and walked towards the pub entrance. I knew instinctively that it was Susan. I didn't want her to have to sit there on her own, so I followed her in and introduced myself.

Unlike the huge emotional scenes you see on TV our first meeting was very awkward; we just looked at each other, neither of us knowing what to say. Susan broke the ice by commenting on what a lovely old pub it was, so we talked about its history for a while and then I asked her if she would like something to eat as the food here was very good. We sat talking for hours, and she told me about her life and I told her about mine. I must admit I felt a sense of pride at the way she had turned out, but of course I could take no credit for it. At the end of the evening we agreed to meet again.

Where Alison was concerned, she had always been my only child, and now I had to tell her that in fact I had another daughter. She actually took it quite well, so I thought it would be nice for both of them to meet, as they were after all half-sisters. However, this meeting proved to be a mistake, because Alison, who had never been anything other than a mum, and was happy just being at home, cooking and looking after the kids, was made to feel inferior by Susan, who was well-educated, well-dressed and totally independent. She made no attempt to put Alison at ease and hardly even spoke to her, and it was clear they had nothing in common. I did meet Susan again on several occasions and tried to get close to her, but it never really worked out. I think neither of us saw in the other what we had wanted them to be. We were not like mother and daughter, or even friends. I'm sure she thinks the fault is all down to me, as I suppose most of it is, but she didn't make it easy either. I think when a child has been adopted there is always a certain amount of resentment, regardless of the reason why, and the mother bears that guilt for the rest of her life.

Chapter 7

Israel, and a new life

As the day for my departure got closer, I became more nervous and started to worry if I was doing the right thing. But then that day came, and after all my tearful goodbyes I boarded an El Al plane once again. The plane touched down at Ben Gurion Airport and all of the new immigrants had to wait to be interviewed and have their documents scrutinised, which took hours. It was around two in the morning when I was finally cleared and I still had no idea what part of Israel

I would be going to.

After a long drive which seemed to take forever, I ended up with a couple of other new immigrants at a place called Haifa. We were taken to a building that looked like a college, and after being checked in I was shown to a small room, which I was told was where I would now be staying. I just fell on the bed and slept until the morning. When I awoke I could hear lots of laughing and people going backwards and forwards past my room but I couldn't pluck up the courage to look outside. About seven o'clock a woman called Katyah knocked on my door and said 'I will take you for breakfast and then you can meet the others'.

Breakfast was in a large canteen, and I learned that all future meals would be served here. After breakfast Katyah took me into a room where several other people, boys and girls, were sitting around chatting. We were told to introduce ourselves, give our names and say from which country we were from. Most of the people were younger than me and there was only one other person from England. Most of them were from America, but there were also people from Canada, Australia, Brazil, Yemen, Iraq, and various other countries that I can't remember. Katyah explained that the building we were in was called an 'ulpan', which is like a university campus, and there we would live and be taught until we got a job, or decided which part of the country we wanted to live in permanently. We were told that we could spend the first week getting to know the area and getting to know each other, but then we must start Hebrew classes in earnest.

We were split into different groups according to our knowledge of Hebrew, so of course I was in the beginners' class. I found Hebrew very difficult and felt intimidated when some of the group who started with me were already streets ahead. Stupidly I dropped out of the class and spent the days travelling around the country going to archaeological digs and places of historical interest. But the evenings were really fun, because we all used to gather in each other's rooms and play music until the early hours – it was like being a teenager again.

It was at the ulpan that I made friends with an American woman called Gerda and we remained best friends for the next twenty-three years. But all good things come to an end. After being at the ulpan for a year the financial assistance from the Israeli Government ran out and I realised I had to get a job. I loved the stunning beauty of Haifa, but I knew I would never get a job there when I was unable to speak or understand Hebrew. I was now painfully aware of how I had wasted this first year.

Although the Israeli Government no longer supported living expenses at the ulpan when the year was up, it did give new immigrants a loan with very low interest to enable them to rent or buy an apartment. One of the American students was a lawyer, and he helped me with all the forms and paperwork, so I set about looking for a place to live. Gerda left before me, and was renting a tiny apartment just on the outskirts of Jerusalem. I decided that Tel Aviv was my best bet, because almost everybody spoke English. The prices in Tel Aviv were very high because it is a thriving city with loads of offices and businesses and shops. All the embassies were in Tel Aviv, even though Jerusalem is the capital city. I was unable to afford any of the apartments that I looked at first, but it was possible with the loan and the money I had brought with me to buy a 'key money apartment'. This was a scheme (now abolished) where you buy a third of the value of the apartment and pay a very small amount in rent. It is never actually yours, but you have the security that you cannot be evicted and you get the original amount paid back when you leave.

Key money apartments are usually very old properties in less desirable areas that often need a lot of work doing on them. However, I was really fortunate to find an apartment in Allenby Street, right in the centre of Tel Aviv, opposite the famous Carmel Market, and close to all the shops and bus stops which wasn't in too bad a state. The furniture left by the previous tenant was pretty disgusting, but I couldn't afford to buy new furniture just yet. My first priority was to find a job.

I spent a couple of weeks getting to know the area where I was now living, and brought the *Jerusalem Post,* which is a daily paper in English covering most of the country. There were several companies seeking accountants in the Tel Aviv area with a good knowledge of English. One of the companies advertising was in an office block about ten minutes from where I lived, so I thought I would try that one first. The block was an impressive building situated across the street from the American Embassy, and next to several banks. I noticed that the entire block belonged to one insurance company, so I walked through the huge doors and asked to see someone about the vacancy. After the receptionist made a phone call a young girl came down the stairs and asked me to follow her. I was interviewed by the office manager and someone from the personnel department. I explained that my Hebrew wasn't good but they said 'Don't worry, you will soon pick it up'. I had my doubts about that, considering I had only picked up three or four words in the year I had spent at Haifa.

Instead of the usual 'we will let you know' I was told straight away I had the job and could start on Sunday. It took me some time to get used to the week starting on Sunday, but I fell into the work routine quite quickly. Like the ulpan, there were people from other parts of the world working in the various offices as well as those born in Israel. In the office I was put in, I was working next to an American guy called Ephraim and we soon became close friends. The work I was responsible for involved reconciling all the overseas business, checking the invoices and preparing them for payment, as well as chasing up money owed to us. It was practically the same work I had done for Frank, so I found it easy. However, the working hours were very hard; work started at 7.30 am and didn't finish until 4.30 pm, sometimes even later. There was no official lunch hour – you brought in your own food and ate it at your desk – but there were coffee and tea machines, so we could drink as much as we wanted.

I found it difficult at first organising myself around the Israeli week, as all the shops closed from Friday noon to Saturday evening and all the public transport stopped as well. This meant I had to do shopping for food etc after finishing work. But even when there was no public transport there was a taxi service called a 'sherut' which wasn't very expensive.

I thought that after living in England I would love the sun, but I found the heat and humidity very difficult to cope with. After months and months of boiling heat day after day with no air or breeze, I started to pray for rain. Shops, offices and transport had very good air conditioning, but my apartment, being very old, had none, so cooking and housework were a nightmare.

I soon built up a social life with the people I worked with, and a group of us often met up in the evenings to go for a meal in any of the numerous cafés and coffee shops that stayed open as long as there was a customer. And because Israel was a melting pot for people from almost every country in the world, the choice of food was extensive.

When I wasn't staying at home in Tel Aviv for the weekend I would take the bus to Jerusalem and stay with Gerda. Jerusalem was incredibly beautiful and full of history, but although we both loved walking around the old city and visiting sites connected with the bible, I never felt completely comfortable there. Gerda would sometimes come and stay with me in Tel Aviv, and she couldn't get over how laid back it was in comparison to Jerusalem.

It was in September, the hottest time of the year, just before the holiday of Rosh Hashanah (Jewish New Year) that a very strange thing happened. I was preparing to visit Gerda and was packing a small case, and I had to keep stopping because the heat was so unbearable and stifling. All of a sudden, the front door, which was locked and bolted, burst open, and a freezing cold chill surrounded me. The hairs stood up on my arms, and I had a terrifying feeling that something unnatural was in the room. I started shaking and had to sit down to compose myself, when the phone rang. Before I answered it I knew it would be my father. 'Mummy has just died' he sobbed 'you must come home' I have never told anyone about this before, because it is something I can't explain, but I will never forget it.

I arranged to fly to England as soon as I could, which was very difficult at such short notice. I then took the ferry to the Isle of Wight. When I reached my parents' home my father was inconsolable and incapable of doing anything, so it was left to me to arrange the funeral as my sister and her husband were in America.

I then got another shock. My mother, who had been far more orthodox than my father and spoke in Yiddish when at home, had left instructions that she wanted a small cross put into her coffin along with the Star of David she always wore. I couldn't believe it. Who was she? But it was her wish, for whatever reason, so I had to abide by it. The saddest thing was that my father and I and one neighbour were the only people at her funeral.

I stayed with my father until my sister got back from America and then returned to Israel. On the flight back I thought about my mother a great deal. I felt so sad that she had died almost alone, and that she had kept so many secrets from my sister and me. She could have had a good life with her daughters, yet she had died without even knowing her grandchildren. My mother had two sayings that she repeated constantly. One was 'when poverty walks through the door, love flies out the window', and the other was 'money might not make you happy, but at least you can be miserable in comfort'. I don't know why these sayings came into my head, but they were so typical of her.

As well as my friends from work I made new friends with a pair of sisters from Manchester who also lived in Tel Aviv. They were both hairdressers and our friendship began when they started to do my hair. I had just got a little dog called Poppy from a rescue home, and they also had a dog, so we often took them for long walks together along the beach. Walking a dog is a wonderful way of getting to know the history of a place and of meeting people. I would take Poppy out before going to work and again in the evening. So through walking up and down the same streets on a regular basis I got to know all the shopkeepers, who would often come out to stroke Poppy and talk to me. But whereas in England I was the 'Jew girl', here in Tel Aviv I was now the 'English woman'.

I had been working in the insurance company for more than two years when the company moved to Ramat Gan, so I now had to travel back and forth by bus, which meant I had to leave earlier and get back later. Although I had still not managed to speak Hebrew except for a few words, most of my Israeli colleagues now spoke perfect English.

The following Rosh Hashanah my father had a stroke, and he died on the exact same day two years after my mother. This time my sister arranged the funeral and he was buried next to my mother. It was what he had wanted, but I doubt if it would have been what my mother wanted. The proceeds of the sale of the bungalow were left to me as it was in my mother's will, but it didn't amount to very much because my parents had not kept it in good order. There was a lot of money owing that had to be settled and what was left I split with my sister. When the money was released I had my apartment redecorated, which it badly needed, and bought a new bed and furniture.

Each Christmas I returned to England to see my daughter and grandchildren. My daughter now had three children, but the two younger ones hardly knew me. It was very emotional, because I wanted to be part of their lives, but when I was in England I missed my life in Israel. Unfortunately, when you are born in one country and then live in another, you are always torn between the two, because you can never shake off your past; you carry it with you wherever you go. I have always been proud of being English and of being born in London, and cherished what used to be thought of as British values, but every time I returned, I found that the England that I had left behind was gradually eroding away. Shops like Timothy Whites & Taylors, C&A, Suitors and Woolworths were all gone. Now it's all charity shops and pound shops, and most of the beautiful countryside is now housing estates, which is very sad. The authorities don't seem to realise how dangerous it is to get rid of the woodlands and destroy the wildlife. Badgers, foxes, birds and reptiles are disappearing at an alarming rate. It seems that nothing has a right to live other than humans

On returning to Tel Aviv I soon dropped back into the social scene. I still regularly met my friends from the office for falafel or hummus after work in Dizengov, and when I wasn't visiting Gerda in Jerusalem at weekends or visiting friends on their kibbutz, I would take Poppy with me to have Friday night dinner with my hairdressing friends.

The Passover holiday was coming up and Gerda was on holiday in America, so I was determined to fulfil my lifelong dream of going to Egypt. I had studied Egyptology for years and had taken a course in hieroglyphs, which unfortunately I soon forgot. This was the best time for me to go, but it angered one of the religious men in the office, who remarked, 'the whole of Israel is celebrating coming out of Egypt, so you decide it's the time to go back in'. I didn't plan it on purpose to coincide with Passover – it was just a convenient time off work. As I said before, I am proud of my Jewish heritage but I am not religious, for me it's the history and the culture. So ignoring the comments, I took the bus down to Eilat, and from there I went to Egypt by coach. I still had a British passport, and although relationships between Israel and Egypt were cool, it was still possible to go there. However, I was advised not to use my Israeli passport.

Crossing the border was a nightmare. We were left hanging around for a couple of hours in the boiling heat, and then we were ripped off over the money exchange. I decided that the next time I came I would choose a different way of entering the country.

My first view of Egypt was mind-blowing. You

see pictures of the pyramids in books, on television and in films and although you know exactly what they look like, when they actually come in to view, it is awesome. I booked in at a hotel close to the Cairo museum and made it my first port of call. The museum was amazing but slightly disorganised. I bought a brochure to find my way around, and found that some of the exhibits were wrongly named. I must admit that the Tutankhamen exhibition was beautifully laid out, but the main reason I had come was to see the huge statues of the eighteenth dynasty Pharaoh Akhenaten. Since the very first book I read about him by James Henry Breasted in my early teens, I have been obsessed with Akhenaten and the Amarna period. He was the very first monotheist, long before Judaism, Christianity or Islam. When the entire ancient world was worshipping hundreds of different gods, this man decreed that there was only one god, the Aten. Now here I was gazing up at him in the same way as his subjects would have done over three and a half thousand years ago. I had only a couple of days left in Egypt, which I spent at the museum and decided that I had to come back.

As well as my usual friends in Tel Aviv I also had a few boyfriends, all much younger than me, but I never took them seriously; I suppose it was just an ego booster after my three failed marriages. It really felt like I was living a charmed life, and I had never been so happy. But as always, whenever things seemed to be going well there was always something bad waiting to happen. Since being in Israel I had lost my mother and my father, and next it was my son-in-law Peter, who died of a heart attack in his early thirties. I know I tried to stop Alison from marrying him as I was sure he was a womaniser and would knock her about, but even so I wouldn't have wished this on him. My heart went out to Alison and the children.

Once again, I had to hurriedly arrange a flight

back to England. Fortunately, Alison was surrounded by family and friends, which was a comfort to her. I don't know who arranged the funeral, but it was an eye-opening experience. When we awoke in the morning the entire area was covered with men standing together in rows. There must have been over a hundred, and Alison hardly knew any of them. Peter was a gypsy by birth and it was their tradition that when one of them died they would come from all over the country to show their respect. Even on the way to the funeral at Iver in Buckinghamshire, the traffic was brought to a halt as lorry after lorry passed by piled with flowers. It was certainly a funeral I will never forget.

I stayed with Alison for a while, but she said she was all right as her cousin was staying with her and her father was close by. So I returned to Israel to catch up on my work and to collect Poppy from my friends, and soon got back into my usual routine.

The following summer I decided to go back to Egypt. I know I said I wouldn't go down by coach again but I did, because it was the cheapest way. However, this time I was met at the border by Nabil, the taxi driver I had used the last time, and I knew he was trustworthy. I booked into the same hotel close to the museum, and Nabil suggested that if I wanted to see the Karnak temple and visit the tombs in Luxor the best way to go was by the overnight train from Cairo to Luxor. This proved to be a brilliant idea because sleeping on the train saved paying for a room at the hotel.

I reached Luxor at 6.30 am, before it started to get too hot, and it gave me plenty of time to visit Karnak and cross over the Nile to see the best tombs. If you have never been to the Valley of the Kings you can never understand what an awe-inspiring experience it is. To look at the magnificent artwork painted and carved by people with simple tools over five thousand years ago and still just as beautiful today.

After seeing all I wanted to see I returned on the overnight train the same way as I had come. Back in Cairo I visited the museum again, but I desperately wanted to see Amarna, which had been called Akhetaten (Horizen of the Aten) in Akhenaten's time. In the early 1980s there was no means of getting there, so I asked Nabil if he would take me. He said it would be very difficult, because it was such a long way away and he didn't know how to get there, but if I really wanted to go I would have to be up about 5.30 in the morning to allow us to get there and back the same day.

I met Nabil as suggested the next morning and it was pitch black. He had brought a thermos of coffee, some sandwiches and a map and we started off. After driving for about an hour we left the road and were now on a dirt track. Nabil said he had no idea where we were, so he stopped the car to look at the map with the torch. The next thing we knew was flood lights beaming on us and being surrounded by armed soldiers.

I glanced at Nabil, who was sweating and looked terrified. One of the men dragged him out and started pulling everything out of the car. When they pulled me out I was even more terrified than Nabil. We were then driven to a hut and pushed down on a seat. Two of the men were screaming at poor Nabil, but of course I didn't know what they were saying. Then one of the men came to me and tried to take my bag. I shouted 'How dare you! I'm a British archaeologist, is this how you treat people who have come to help you? Give me a phone, I want to speak with the British Embassy.'

This was total nonsense of course, but when you fear your life's in danger, you pull what you can out of the bag. And I was getting visions of Midnight Express. Luckily for us but not so lucky for the poor sods they now dragged in, who Nabil later told me, were caught trafficking drugs, because it took the attention away from us. I could hear them screaming as several of the men were kicking and punching them and it made me feel sick, but at the same time I was relieved it wasn't us.

Then a senior officer who spoke excellent English came over to me and said 'My apologies madam, my men are ignorant and I'm sorry you and your driver have been inconvenienced.' He then tried to catch me out by asking me questions on Ancient Egypt to which I'm sure he didn't know the answers himself. But he was satisfied, and he gestured to two of the soldiers to escort us back to the car. They then put everything back in the car as it was, shook Nabil's hand and told him the best way to get to Amarna, before shouting to me 'Enjoy your stay in Egypt.'

I felt so sorry that I had got Nabil into this, as he had not wanted to go in the first place. I asked him why we had been treated in this way. He said that because it was so dark he had driven by mistake into a security zone, and we were lucky to have got out at all. We drove the rest of the way mostly in silence. We were both very shaken up and I decided that this would be my last visit, even though I loved the country so much.

We finally reached Amarna several hours later than anticipated, only to find there was almost nothing to see. It had been completely demolished in antiquity and now all that remained were the rock-cut boundary stelae and some piles of stones indicating where palaces and temples had once stood. Apart from the huts that people were living in along the river bank, it was just a vast desert. I was disappointed that there was nothing much to see, but still thrilled to be standing on the site where a thriving city filled with magnificent palaces and temples had once stood, and to imagine Akhenaten and Nefertiti driving by in their horse-drawn chariots. Now, many years after that visit, I follow all the archaeology carried out at Amarna on the television and I so badly wish that I could be there.

On my return to Israel life carried on pretty much as before, but I was getting older and found the heat harder and harder to cope with. My apartment was on the top storey with no lift, and carrying heavy shopping up the stairs became more difficult. I was still unable to hold a conversation in Hebrew and started to worry about my health. Both my parents had died of strokes, and I began to worry about what would happen to me if I had a stroke and was unable to call for help.

Then during the 'Scuds war' it was a very scary time, as it wasn't known if they were carrying chemicals or not. The whole of the country was told to make sealed rooms and we were all issued with gas masks. As soon as it started to get dark the Scuds started landing, so you had to make sure whenever you were out that you could get back in time. Several Scuds hit Tel Aviv, but luckily nobody got killed. A lot of Israelis moved to Eilat, where it was safer, but I wouldn't leave Poppy. She was so clever I'm sure she understood what was going on, and as soon as she heard the siren she would rush into my bedroom, which was my sealed room. It was during this time that my lack of Hebrew became a real problem, because I couldn't understand what was going on, or the instructions given on television. However, the 'war' only lasted for a couple of months and things soon got back to normal.

I was now nearing retiring age, but because I was so good at my job, I was kept on, and I could have carried on working for another couple of years. But I had now been at the same job for more than twenty years, longer than any of the managers, and I was getting bored. My daughter had met another man and had started another family. And I started to wonder – 'what am I doing here? Am I going to die here alone?'

There had been many deaths since I moved to Israel and they were all upsetting, but the one that affected me the most was when my little dog Poppy got run over. She was the sweetest little dog and the best companion I have ever had. I was devastated, and have never got over it, even today. Without her, life felt empty. I no longer enjoyed going for walks, and the apartment wasn't home any more. So I gave in my notice at work and decided to return to England.

I got mixed comments when I told my friends I was thinking of returning to England. Some of them said 'Yes, Carole, you should be with your family', while others said 'Don't be a fool, your life is here'. But I had made my mind up. I had to sell my share of the apartment back to the solicitors who owned it, and my original payment was now worthless.

When the time came to say goodbye to all my friends I started to have my doubts about leaving, but it was too late to change my mind. The time I spent in Israel was the happiest period of my life, and the people I still call my friends I will never forget.

So I boarded an El Al plane to return to England and cried the whole way. I stayed for the first six months with my daughter and the children, but it was terribly overcrowded. Eventually the council gave me a lovely little one-room flat just on the edge of Burnham in Buckinghamshire. When the weather permits I like to sit on my balcony and watch the birds flitting from tree to tree, or watch the squirrels, they are so entertaining, and I often see foxes in the evening. I love British wildlife and the countryside and feel very lucky to be living here. I see my daughter almost every day, we go shopping together and sometimes go for lunch, and I also spend a lot of time with my grandchildren, all the things that my mother missed and could have enjoyed.

I have now been back for more than fifteen years and have made many new friends, although I still keep in contact with my friends in Israel. They are not ageist; if they like you they don't give a damn how old you are, but in England, once you hit fifty or sixty, you are not seen as a person any more, you become invisible. They never think when they see an old woman that she may have once been beautiful, she may have once been loved or lived an interesting life, nor do they ever think when they see an old man hobbling with a stick that he may have once been a hero during the war; he is now just a pensioner, an old fart.

I don't go to the synagogue now as I don't know what to believe any more. After all, religion is only dictated by the place and time in which you were born.

I regret that during my life I have hurt some people along the way, and I regret some of the decisions I have made, but I have loved and been loved. And didn't Tennyson once write, 'It is better to have loved and lost than never to have loved at all?'

Someone once told me that life was like a bowl of stew. You put in meat, onions, carrots, parsnips and spices. Some of the ingredients you like and some you don't, but when they have simmered for long enough you get a delicious meal. Well my life has been a mixture of many ingredients. Some have been wonderful and some have been awful, but after simmering for over eighty years, I think on the whole, it was a tasty meal.

I have been a daughter, a mother, a grandmother and now I'm a great-grandmother, but inside I am still that little girl sitting on the bench at Rickmansworth station, searching the trains in vain for the mother who never came.